Lake Michigan Rock Picker's Guide

Lake Michigan
Rock Picker's Guide

Bruce Mueller
and
Kevin Gauthier

The University of Michigan Press
Ann Arbor

Petoskey Publishing Company
Traverse City

Published in the United States of America by
The University of Michigan Press
And
The Petoskey Publishing Company
Manufactured in the United States of America
♾ Printed on acid-free paper

2010 2009 2008   5 4 3

Library of Congress Cataloging-in-Publication Data

Mueller, Bruce.
    Lake Michigan rock picker's guide / Bruce Mueller and Kevin Gauthier.
    p. cm.
    ISBN-13: 978-0-472-03150-4 (paper : alk. paper)
    ISBN-10: 0-472-03150-3 (paper : alk. paper)
    1. Rocks—Collection and preservation—Michigan, Lake. 2. Rocks—
Michigan, Lake—Guidebooks. 3. Michigan, Lake—Guidebooks.
I. Gauthier, Kevin. II. Title. III. Title: Rock Picker's guide.

QE445.M53M84   2006
552.09774—dc22   2006050167

Contents

Introduction

In the book *The Complete Guide to Petoskey Stones*, my co-author, William Wilde, explained how he as a boy had become interested in Petoskey stones.

My interest in stones began when I found a slab covered with fossils at the age of eight. Neither I nor my father knew what they were, so we consulted a geology professor at a local college. By the time the professor finished with me, I had decided that geologists were detectives who used rocks to peek through the fog of time into worlds that once existed and which were now long gone. I decided to become a geologist.

After the Korean War, the G.I. Bill, a fellowship, and my wife got me through college. I took a job teaching geology and astronomy, and in order to have something useful to do during summer vacations my wife and I started a rock shop near Honor, Michigan. At the shop and at school, people would bring in stones along with the questions for which they genuinely wanted answers. When William Wilde suggested that we write a book to answer those questions, I thought it was a good idea and knew just what questions to answer.

The questions to answer for almost any stone found on any Lake Michigan beach in any state are as follows:

What kind of stone is this?
How old is it?
Where is it from?
How did it get here?
How did it form?
Where can I find a particular type of stone?
How can I polish it?

Not only will this book answer those questions, it will also be a fun guide for families to help explore Lake Michigan.

–Bruce Mueller

My rock collecting journey started when I was nine years old. I spent hours floating on a surfboard near the shoreline of Lake Leelanau looking through a scuba mask at rocks. By age ten, stacks of containers were filled to the brim with my "colorful gems" and had overtaken my bedroom closet. My mother told me to get rid of them or do something with them. So I want to thank my mother for the jump start in my endeavors. And to my father, who was always creating a new piece of rock cutting equipment from what appeared to be junk parts, I am eternally grateful. There are many people from our local rock and mineral club that helped me along the way including the late William Clark and Vic Nielson. Bill taught me how to cut and polish my first cabochon and Vic opened my eyes to the world of crystals. Davidson's, our local rock shop, shared information and tips on polishing, which helped me perfect my art. I want to thank Chenina, my lovely wife, who is always patient and understanding of my passion and long hours dedicated to rockhounding. Finally to our children: Kyle, who collected his first rocks into a baby food jar while watching me on the beach, and Samantha, who is always asking, "Can I help?" in the work shop. I hope you will hold as many fond memories of our rockhounding adventures in your heart as I have.

–Kevin Gauthier

LAKE MICHIGAN'S ROCKS

Type	Stone Hardness
Basalt	6
Brachiopods*	3
Chain coral*	7/3
Chert	7
Cladapora*	3
Copper	3
Crinoids*	3
Diamonds	10
Favosite/Charlevoix*	3
Feldspar	6
Fern Creek tillite	6.5-7
Frankfort green	5.5
Fulgurite	7
Greenstone *(chlorastrolite)*	6.5
Granite	6.5-7
Gold	2.5-3
Gowganda tillite	6.5-7
Horn coral*	3
Honey comb coral*	6.5-7
Jasper	7
Lake Superior agate	7
Leeland blue	5.5
Lightning stones	3.5-4
Marcacite	6-6.5
Misfits	a range
Moonstone	6
Pipe organ coral*	3
Petoskey stones*	3
(Michigan's state stone)	
Pudding stone	6.5-7
Quartz	7
Rhyolite porphyry	6-7
Sandstone	7
Stink stone	3
Trilobite*	3
Unakite	6.5-7

Note: Fossils if replaced by calcite will be 3 in hardness. If replaced by quartz, they will be 7 in hardness. Fossils replaced by dolomite, which is just calcite that contains magnesium, will have a hardness of 3.5-4.

*fossil

Mohs Scale of Hardness		Common Objects Hardness	
Diamond	10		
Corundum (ruby, sapphire)	9	8.5	wet/dry course sand
Topaz	8		paper
Quartz	7		
Feldspar	6	6.5	harden steel (file)
Apatite	5	5	knife blade or glass
Fluorite	4	4	copper (penny date
Calcite	3		1980 or earlier)
Gypsum	2	2.5	fingernail
Talc	1		

Rock Collecting Rules

Keep in mind you are sharing and using the same beaches with many other people. The parks and places mentioned in this book should be treated with respect by following their rules and regulations. The rules for collecting vary from state to state and from park to park. There are national parks, state parks, county parks, township parks, city parks, and there is private property. It's best to check in advance before collecting. In general the more important the park, national or state, the less likely collecting is to be allowed. Some park officials are more lenient than others. Leave a few less rocks for the waves to replenish and only foot prints behind.

For listing of parks see the following web sites:
www.michigandnr.com   www.illiniosdnr.com
www.wisconsondnr.com   www.indianadnr.com
www.parks.state.mi.us

In this picture, on the right is rock debris covered glacial ice of the Coleman Glacier, Mt. Baker, Washington. To the left is rock debris that has dropped from the glacier's melting edge.

This melting and dropping of debris left rocks throughout the Great Lakes (seen here in Sleeping Bear National Lakeshore).

A piece of glacial debris (an eratic) drug over bedrock and scratched (striated) by a glacier. These are fairly common in glacial debris above the lake as in the pile of glacial debris (a moraine) shown at Sleeping Bear on the preceding page.

This 300 pound boulder has had glacial force ground groves into it.

How Lake Michigan Was Formed

Lake Michigan was created by the Wisconsin ice sheet, the last of the great ice sheets to move out of the north during recent time. One lobe of the ice sheet moved into a river valley that occupied a valley where the lake is today. The valley was there because the bedrock was soft shale.

As the glacier moved down the river valley, it drug hard rock along its base, especially granite, that it had picked up in Canada. To the north of the lake lie two million square miles of Canadian Shield; the ancient stable core around which the North American Continent was built. This glacier, which created Lake Michigan, was about a mile and a half thick. At its base the pressure of the overlying ice would have been well in excess of 200 tons per square foot. Both the rock that the glacier was dragging and the shale were ground to dust.

The glacier wasn't a bulldozer, it was a conveyor belt driven by sunlight on the northern hemisphere. Each cubic mile of ice carried a fraction of a cubic mile of rock south, and the glacial conveyor belt flowed south for about 63,000 years. As the glacier moved south it was eroding. The powdered rock, sand, gravel and boulders it carried were dropped to the south, east and west of the lake. As the glacier began to melt back, it deposited the stone it carried in the lake and on its shores.

Stones that the glacier had collected from the north, dropped these small treasures onto the beaches. Some of the rock found at Illinois Beach State Park may have come from the Arctic coast of Canada nearly 2000 miles away, and the glacier collected and deposited rock

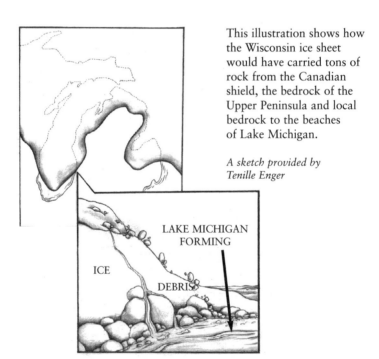

This illustration shows how the Wisconsin ice sheet would have carried tons of rock from the Canadian shield, the bedrock of the Upper Peninsula and local bedrock to the beaches of Lake Michigan.

A sketch provided by Tenille Enger

LAKE MICHIGAN FORMING

ICE

DEBRIS

from everywhere in between. The glacier collected rocks for us from places we could never go and left them on beaches that are practically on our doorstep here in the Midwest. Because of glacial transport of rock from the Canadian Shield, Lake Michigan and the other Great Lakes have more varieties and colors of rock on their beaches than you are likely to find anywhere else on earth. All of this variety and color is part of the charm of Lake Michigan beaches.

> The Great Lakes have more color and variety of stones than anywhere on the planet.

A young rockhound testing the cold spring water

Variety –16 Flavors in a Dixie Cup

On a very warm fourth of July, I was on Old Mission Peninsula off Bluff Road (near Traverse City, Michigan). The beach was sandy and very few rocks washed ashore as the beach faced south east. Prevailing winds can be a factor to rock exposure. That day I was in-charge of watching our children playing in the water – a very busy three-year old girl and a five-year old boy. Since it was such a hot day I decided to build a sand castle at the water's edge to keep my feet in the cool water. As I dug down, I hit a layer of very small rocks about dime size. The rocks were always there but I believe the current must have buried these rocks with about six inches of sand. Before I realized it, I was on a rock-hunting trip, one that took no effort to walk anywhere. Digging between my legs, I carefully studied each rock. That day I got a real feel for the variety of rocks that could be collected on Lake Michigan. In an hour I dug a one-foot circle, about a foot deep, filling only a Dixie cup. The best part about this rock trip was the carrying of the stones. A year later I decided to take a tally of the "pretty" rocks I found that day.

In that Dixie cup I had found:

4   red jasper

13   granite stones with colors varying from red, yellow, black, green, and pink

2   limestone (one was foot shaped)
1   basalt with green epidot lines
1   yellow granite with epidot lines running through
6   Petoskey stones
17 favosite fossils
1   crinoid stem fossil (notice the eye ball resemblance)
1   branch coral
1   sand stone - burgundy in color
1   black basalt
2   feldspar
4   pieces of tan chert
1   flint chip (that looked like it could have come
    from working an arrow head)
18 transparent quartz (60% of the earth's surface
    is quartz, much of which is sand)
3   Lake Superior agates (two chips and one whole
    nugget with distinctive eye banding)
    (See color photos 2, 3.)

All of this in a one foot circle which I had thought was only a sandy beach! When I found the rocks, my priorities changed very quickly. The kids ended up with a very small sand castle and I was reprimanded to keep a better eye on the kids next time.

A curious rock hunter

Canadian rock is easy to recognize. You won't be able to scratch it with a knife blade. If it has flattened or elongated crystals or alternating dark and light bands of minerals, it is metamorphic. Otherwise, with a few negligible exceptions (such as chert), it is igneous. If the rock can be scratched with a knife (with the exception of chert), it is bedrock from the Upper Peninsula, or much more likely from the bedrock where you are or from just offshore.

Just Three Sources for Lake Michigan Rocks

It's hard to tell in advance whether a beach will be grassy, sandy or covered with stone; but it's relatively easy to know what the stone will be if it's a stony beach. There are just three sources for beach stone: The Canadian Shield, sedimentary rock from further north and local sedimentary rock. The Canadian Shield rock will be present in greater or lesser quantities on every stony beach; it's a given. If you know what the sedimentary rock to the north is and what the local bedrock is, you know in advance what types of rocks there will be at a particular beach.

A Trip around Lake Michigan–
Understanding the Bedrock

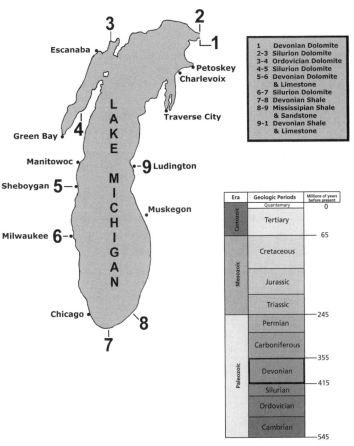

1	Devonian Dolomite
2-3	Silurion Dolomite
3-4	Ordovician Dolomite
4-5	Silurion Dolomite
5-6	Devonian Dolomite & Limestone
6-7	Silurion Dolomite
7-8	Devonian Shale
8-9	Mississipian Shale & Sandstone
9-1	Devonian Shale & Limestone

Era	Geologic Periods	Millions of years before present
Cenozoic	Quanternary	0
Cenozoic	Tertiary	
Cenozoic		65
Mesozoic	Cretaceous	
Mesozoic	Jurassic	
Mesozoic	Triassic	
Mesozoic		245
Paleozoic	Permian	
Paleozoic	Carboniferous	
Paleozoic		355
Paleozoic	Devonian	
Paleozoic		415
Paleozoic	Silurian	
Paleozoic	Ordovician	
Paleozoic	Cambrian	
Paleozoic		545

The Geologic Timeline

Point # 1- Bedrock near Fort Michilimackinac, MI

To start a bedrock trip around the lake, a good place to begin is at the south end of the Big Mac Bridge at the top of the Lower Peninsula (point one on the map).

If we start there, we will save the best for last. If you stop at Mackinaw City and park under the bridge near Fort Michilimackinac and go down to the lake, the gravel you will find there is Devonian dolomite. This dolomite was shattered to a fine gravel called breccia when the underlying water-soluble rock dissolved away and the overlying dolomite collapsed into the void. All of this happened hundreds of millions of years ago and its probable collapses occurred repeatedly.

Most people who like to collect fossils like to collect large, splendid, well-preserved specimens; but there are no large specimens here, only gravel. The gravel does contain many fossils but with few exceptions, none is well preserved. While you're there under the bridge, Fort Michilimackinac is worth seeing.

Point # 2- Bedrock near St. Ignace, MI

On the other side of the bridge (at point 2 on the map), the rock is dolomite of Silurian age. It's called Niagaran dolomite because this is the layer over which Niagara Falls falls. There are generally few, if any, worthwhile fossils in dolomite. Sometimes there are interesting, even rare, fossils in dolomite, but the preservation leaves something to be desired. When you find other stony beaches in the Upper Peninsula, they will have stones similar to those found near Brevort. If you take Route 2 from the toll booth on the north end of the Big Mac Bridge, you will pass miles and miles of excellent sandy swimming beaches, which during the hot days of summer will be swarming with people swimming and getting a sun tan. Everyone just parks right along the road and goes down to the beach.

A stony beach near Brevort in the Upper Peninsula

Silurian Niagaran dolomite at Fayette on the Garden Peninsula of the Upper Peninsula

19.2 miles from the bridge toll booth, and about two miles east of a little town called Brevort, you will see a scenic overlook sign on the lake side of the road. At the end of the road there is a stairway leading down to the lake. This is an exceptionally nice beach. It is covered with glacial gravel, most of it from either the Silurian or Ordovician bedrock that lies to the north in the Upper Peninsula, and with colorful stones from Canada. Here there are many large fossil coral colonies.

There are at least five or six different coral species here. There is chert, some of it perhaps gunflint chert from Canada. There is banded chert here, turitella-like snail shells and hornblend schist. There is also Michigan moonstone, we found two low quality Lake Superior agates, mottled chert, chain coral, favosites and the usual basalt, granite and quartz. If it's about lunch time you might eat in Brevort, as there are a couple of nice restaurants there. You can also find the very famous pasties all around this area and throughout the Upper Peninsula.

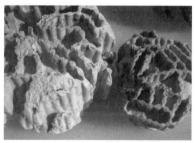

A pristine chain coral head–has had no wave action

Point # 3 - Bedrock near Escanaba, MI

The rest of the Upper Peninsula (west to the shore of Green Bay, north of Escanaba) is mostly relatively barren Niagaran dolomite or sand.

Look for Cut River Park at Cut River Bridge. There is nice scenery and there are great trees here, but it's 231 steps by stairway down to the lake. At the lake you will find igneous, metamorphic and dolomite boulders too big to pick up. Driving south along the shore of Green Bay, the water is very shallow, dolomite bedrock is exposed almost everywhere except where it is covered by sand. There is little or no glacial gravel.

Driving north on the west shore of Door County, the bedrock continues dolomite, but here the water offshore is deeper and the prevailing wind blows onshore, generating better waves. Along this shore are places where the lake is accessible by road. The rock on the beach contains Canadian gravel, but not much. The rock here is primarily broken cobbles of dolomite washed clean by wave action. There are brachiopods and corals here along with many other fossils.

About 2 miles east of Dykesville on Route 57 there is a small park and boat launch. The road cuts through a cliff where great blocks of dolomite have fallen off. The surfaces of these blocks are covered with raised, irregular marks called fucoids. These are what remains of trails and tunnels on and in the mud of the sea floor created by unknown organisms.

Wisconsin's State Fossil
The most commonly found Silurian trilobite is Calamene.

Point # 4 - Bedrock near Dykesville, WI

Niagaran Silurian dolomite is a very white dolomite, the same dolomite that is seen at Fayette on the Garden Peninsula. Driving to the point of the Door County Peninsula and south along its east side, it's all Niagaran dolomite, and the shores are nearly free of Canadian gravel. Not until you get to Algoma, near the base of the east side of the peninsula, do you see much Canadian gravel. Right in the middle of town there is glacial gravel and sand, which I suspect was hauled in by trucks to create a decent beach.

South of Algoma at Point Beach State Park there is much glacial gravel, but it is mostly buried by sand. To the south between Two Rivers and Manitowoc, the road parallels the lake and many parking places are provided. Here you will find stones from Canada along with fossils from the Upper Peninsula.

To the south, north of Cleveland, is Fisher Creek State Park. Here, there is a nice deposit of Canadian rock and rock from the Upper Peninsula. My wife and I found tillite (probably from near Norway, Michigan), two low quality Lake Superior agates and several septarian concretions, banded chert, porphyry, rhyolite and the usual igneous and metamorphic Canadian stones.

How do I know if I have a "good" agate?
Agates can be graded many different ways. Primarily the contrast between colors and intense banding will yield a higher dollar value. Also to be considered is the transparency or milkiness of the stone. How rare the type of agate is also can be a big factor. Buying bulk Lake Superior agates should set you back around $8-$20/lb. Most of the bulk agate sold comes from Minnesota gravel pits. The Gem Shop in Cedarburg, Wisconsin, has some very nice agates, and it is well worth a visit if you are traveling near this area.

Point # 5 - Bedrock near Sheboygan, WI

The bedrock here is Devonian dolomite. Just to the south is Kohler-Andrae State Park. There is little here other than sand on the beaches. At Harrington Beach State Park, north of Port Washington, dolomite was quarried and shipped south for use as a flux in the steel mills. A pier made of stone taken from the quarry was built out into the lake for loading the dolomite into ships. This stony pier remnant can still be seen to the south along the beach. The quarry itself is abandoned and filled with water.

Point # 6 - Bedrock near Milwaukee, WI

At Eastbrook Park, just off the lake on the Milwaukee

River, there is Devonian rock with Devonian fossils, mostly bryozoans, crinoids and brachiopods. At Kenosha the beaches are about 100 feet wide and alternate between sand and gravel. Big diamonds were found in Wisconsin, so don't forget to keep an eye out!

21.25 carat diamond found near Milwaukee, Wisconsin! Diamonds are found in a path two hundred miles wide that runs from Iowa on the west to Ohio on the east. The largest diamonds have been found in Wisconsin near Milwaukee. The largest that I know of, a 21 and a quarter carat diamond, was found near Theresa, Wisconsin. One found near Eagle, Wisconsin, in the southeast part of the state, weighed almost 16 carats.

Illinois Beach State Park

Near Zion, Illinois, is Illinois Beach State Park. There are seven miles of beach here with an obsolete nuclear reactor in the middle. Unconfirmed rumors say it contains radioactive material. I hope they locked the door when they left. On this beach there is metaconglomerate, probably from near Norway, Michigan. There is also jasper from the U.P., banded quartzite, and rhyolite porphyry from the floor of Lake Superior, basalt with gas cavities filled with calcite, pebbles filled with crinoid

The beach at Illinois Beach State Park with abandoned
nuclear generator in background

stems, breccia (shattered rock glued together with calcite), chert, quartz, jasper, granite, local Niagaran
dolomite, black basalt and phylite (a metamorphic rock
containing mica). And there is porphyritic basalt and
metamorphosed porphyritic basalt, along with other

Bedding planes typical of sedimentary rock in Ordovician
dolomite. Galena dolomite near Rockford, Illinois.
If it has bedding planes it is sedimentary.

stones of lesser interest, as well as some God-only-knows-what-they-are stones.

As you round the south end of the lake on Route 80 through Chicago, you will see as you near the City of Thornton, rock on both sides of the road that slopes toward you away from a quarry ahead. You will next cross a monster dolomite quarry, one of the largest you are ever likely to see. Don't even think about going there – they won't let you in. As you pass through the other side of the quarry, the rock layers will all slope away from the quarry. This is, again, more Niagaran dolomite. The quarry is in the middle of a reef that grew near the edge of the Silurian Sea. The dolomite is used as a flux in the smelting of steel in Chicago and Gary. There are two such reefs in Illinois, four in Indiana and eight in Wisconsin. When these reefs were growing they were about 20 degrees south of the Equator. Continental Drift has since moved these reefs to about 42 degrees north.

Point # 7 - Bedrock near Gary, IN

Going south on Interstate 94 you will come to a string of parks making up the Indiana Dunes National Lake Shore. Miller Beach at Gary, Indiana, is the furthest beach to the west. Next, to the east is the Indiana Dunes National Lakeshore, then Indiana Dunes State Park, then Michigan City's Washington Park, then northeast to New Buffalo Harbor Park, and finally north to Warren Dunes State Park. Altogether there are more than 42 miles of beach.

This stretch of beach is interrupted by three miles of steel mills. Here there is bedrock other than Niagaran dolomite. The bedrock is shale of late Devonian to early Mississippi age. The shale itself contains few fossils, but there are crinoid stems and fossil corals, probably from lime stones interbedded with the shale.

Point # 8 – Bedrock near St. Joseph, MI

Except for a small patch of Devonian rock just south of St. Joseph, the bedrock is Mississippian shale and sandstone and continues to be Mississippian to Ludington. At South Haven, Michigan, there is a very small park called Deer Lick Creek Park. To get there, take the Blue Star Highway to 76th and 13th Ave. Here the bedrock is shale. The beach and lake floor here is littered with clay ironstone concretions. We found 25 in about 25 minutes. These consist of clay cemented into an iron mineral called siderite. They become highly fractured and the fractures fill with calcite brought in by ground water. The result is what are locally called lightning stones because the calcite forms lightning-like patterns on a dark background. The smaller ones have the most colorful patterns and are sometimes cut for jewelry. To the south is Van Buren State Park. Here, there is rock and septarians (fracture filled with calcite) just offshore. To the north they are present on the beaches at Saugatuck.

Further north in Holland very large septarians, up to

thirty or forty pounds, can be found. Not so much along the lakeshore, which is mostly a concrete wall, but rather in the dirt excavated for building foundations. The tops of some of these stones are full of fossil brachiopods. These concretions are collected and shipped to Japan, where oddly shaped stones are much loved.

Septarian concretions from South Haven, Michigan

Four septarian concretions on the beach at South Haven

Point # 9 - Bedrock near Ludington, MI, Traverse City, MI, Petoskey, MI

To the north of Muskegon the bedrock is sandstone, which contributes little interest to the beach rock. From Ludington, to just north of Petoskey, there begins to be an appreciable amount of glacial debris from the local limestone. The bedrock along the lake is limestone and shale, much of it full of beautifully preserved fossils, especially fossil corals. Some of the more common fossil corals include: Petoskey stones, favosite fossils, horn

corals, honeycomb corals, pipe organ corals, crinoids, brachiopods, cephalopods, clams, snails and rarely a trilobite
or two are also found. In addition to the variety of fossils
there is a large amount of Canadian rock intermixed with
the fossils. This lends a wide variety of color to these
beaches. Petoskey stones glacially transported from the
Devonian rocks north of Manistee are abundant enough
at Muskegon to encourage people to actively seek them
there. The further north you go, the more you will find.

On M-22 from Manistee heading toward Frankfort,
there are several obvious places (scenic overlooks, etc.) from
which it is possible to reach the beach. South of Frankfort
there is Elberta Municipal Beach, and to the south there is
a long, high bank beach. I have seen one very beautiful septarian concretion found here that probably came from the
U.P. I have also seen a Devonian armor plated fish that was
found here. Near Crystal Lake and Frankfort there is access
to the lake at Point Betsie Lighthouse.

I think that there must be at least 10,000 people who
walk this beach every summer. Despite this, Lake
Michigan seems to replenish the beaches' supply of
Petoskey stones every year. At Sleeping Bear Dunes
National Lakeshore there is no collecting allowed. Just
beyond the Dunes is Leland, and there is beach access and
good collecting to the north. If you take 201 North
beyond Northport, you will come to Peterson Park, an
excellent place for a picnic lunch. This park sits on a high
bank (about ten stories up) overlooking Lake Michigan. If

you get lucky, on a clear day and at the right time you can view the Great Lake freighters in distant shipping lanes. There is access to the lake, but it is a hike coming up, about 100 stairs. Further north on 201 is DeLong Road which leads to Christmas Cove Road, which leads to Cathead Point. If you are this far, you might as well go all the way to the point and visit the lighthouse or Nature Gems in Northport.

Grand Traverse Bay

The east side of Grand Traverse Bay, north of Traverse City, is heavily populated, making it difficult to reach the shoreline here. The west side of Grand Traverse Bay is protected from strong wave action by the Leelanau Peninsula and is also heavily populated. On the Leelanau Peninsula the west side beaches are, for the most part, high bank areas. The beach can be reached at the tip of the peninsula at Leelanau State Park and Grand Traverse Lighthouse.

North of Traverse City the beach can be reached at Barnes County Park near Eastport. In the Village of Torch Lake there is, just about in the center of town, a road labeled Nature Preserve that leads to a beach called Grandma's Beach.

Barnes County Park near Eastport holds a Petoskey Stone Festival in early summer. For more information see www. Petoskeystonefestival.com

Stony beach at Grandma's Beach near Torch Lake Village

If you travel on U.S. 31 to Richardson Road near Atwood and follow it to the Old Dixie Highway and go south on the Old Dixie Highway, a road toward the lake will lead to Banks Township Park, from which it is possible to walk north to Norwood. There are fossil corals

Giant concretions near Norwood, Michigan.
Stone on the beach is shale bedrock.

here but not many. The bedrock here is shale, and you will see shale torn up all over the beach. About a half mile north there is a large group of concretions on the beach and in the water. These stones grew within the shale as the shale was being compressed, and it is easy to see how the shale was deformed by their growth. The concretions are composed of a variety of oil-rich calcite called anthraconite, also known as cone-in-cone. They give this stretch of beach an other-worldly appearance. Fragments of these concretions scattered elsewhere along the lake are often mistaken for petrified wood. These geodes are worthless, but they do dress up this stretch of beach. Please do not disturb them or try to smash other rocks on them. These are there for picture taking only.

The shale in this area, especially north of Norwood, infrequently contains rare armor-plated Devonian fossil fish and fish fragments. In the outcrops of Antrim Shale it is also possible to find marcasite nodules. They form in the layers of the shale. If you go in early spring, the ice will break up the shale and do the work for you. I have seen some perfectly well-preserved snail fossils found in this area. There is beach access also at the city park in Norwood and Fisherman's Island State Park near Charlevoix. There will be many fossil coral and banded chert along the way.

Further north is Petoskey, Michigan. Because the city of Petoskey is a hot spot for these corals, they are commonly called Petoskey stones, However, the real name came from Chief Petosgay. Translated from Ottawa (or Odawa) "rays of the rising sun" or "sunbeams of promise."

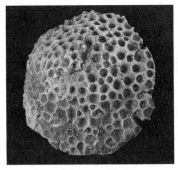 

Hexagonaria coral head
photo courtesy Joe Kchodl

Petoskey stone

Today, there are several great, great, great grandchildren of Chief Petosgay who live and work around the Grand Traverse area. Also, one who lives in South Carolina still attends the annual Pow-Wow in northern Michigan.

Just south of Petoskey is Sunset Park. Here I have picked up a variety of fossils and colorful granites. Just behind the hospital in Petoskey is a park where the beach is also accessible.

I have not done a lot of hunting on the beaches further north, near Good Hart and Cross Village, but I would assume one would find a mixture of Devonian dolomite (which is from where we started at point #1) and granites from Canada (the Canadian Shield).

Anyway by now if you took this entire trip around Lake Michigan, you should have a trunk load of rocks.

Now that you have picked up all these really cool rocks – some with multiple colors, some with different depths of transparences, some stripped, some not, and finally some with bumps and grooves from erosion, how do you know what the rocks really are? What label do you put on them? The next section of this guide should help you do just that.

Did you know Michigan has more state campgrounds than any other state?

Rocks Found on
Lake Michigan Beaches

Basalt

Basalt is the hard, black or dark green rock found on the beach. It is almost always overlooked and really has no character. It is the magma that has cooled near the surface. These rocks were prized by local Indians for hammer stones when breaking flint for making arrowheads. Because of their hardness, they were also used to grind corn and herbs. The characterless basalt will take on some character when veins of quartz and other minerals start to appear in it. (See photos 4,5,6.)

Brachiopods

Brachiopods and a variety of other shells can found throughout the Devonian limestone. It is uncommon to find whole shells, but it is common to find impressions of shells or fragments imbedded in shale and limestone. The horizontal slice of a shell embedded in limestone can look like a single or multiple white "C" shapes in a gray-colored rock. (See photo 7.)

Chain coral

The name describes this stone. Look for a stone with a bunch of chains interlocking. This stone is rare and thus not often found. The top view is easy to identify, and fragments or the side view of a coral will have a tan color with white to cream color lines. The white lines are actually the fossilized coral. The tan part is the filler. This coral was replaced with quartz leaving these white lines always raised up higher than the tan part of the stone. (See photos 8, 9.) It is Silurian in age and from the U.P.

Chert

Chert is microcrystalline quartz. It will come in a variety of colors, but chert is opaque and not transparent. Chert can be one solid color or banded. It can be confused with an agate very easily. I identify chert primarily in two ways: first, by its concoidial fractures, and second, it is not transparent. A third identifier is not as dependable, but it usually will be tan to cream in color and, on rare occasions, tanish red. Near Leland, Michigan, a blue chert can be found; however, it is only surface color (See photos 10, 11.)

Cladopora

Cladopora are branches of coral (formed similar to the bleached white coral you see at pet stores) that have been buried in compressed mud (shale). Cladopora is best described as a staghorn coral. It often occurs as a grey-white coral in a jet black stone saturated with crude oil, which is what gives the stone its color. Cladopora lived during both Silurian and Devonian times, and since it is found on the beach and not in place in bedrock, it's hard to tell whether it is from the Silurian of the Upper Peninsula or the Devonian of the Lower Peninsula. (See photo 12.)

Copper

Native copper, that is pure chunks of copper, can be found in a wide path from Indianapolis, Indiana, on the east to at least as far west as Rockford, Illinois. The only probable source for native copper is the Keweenaw Peninsula, a thumb of land that juts out from the Upper Peninsula of Michigan into Lake Superior. It seems unlikely that much, if any, will be found on the east side of Lake Michigan, but there is undoubtedly some on the west side of the lake. Any large, obvious chunks on the shoreline were picked up long ago, but a metal detector might locate a chunk or two along the lake shore or to the west in the glacial debris. I found two pieces on 7 acres I own near Rockford, Illinois. My neighbor found one, and I own a 69 pound piece found near Madison, Wisconsin. (See photo 13.)

Crinoids

I love this stone! I get more chuckles about the things people have convinced themselves that they have found with this one. Crinoids are relatives of star fish. They had roots like a plant, a stem on top, which had a body with arms. (Star fish seem to be crinoids which have abandoned their roots and stem and taken up a mobile life.) Crinoids are composed of many plates held together by cartilage. At death their plates fell apart almost instantly. Pieces of crinoids are the most common of fossils, a complete crinoid is among the rarest of fossils.When an obscure broken fragment is found - Wow!

People's imagination runs wild, especially if the fragment is at an angle. I have heard people claim, "I have found a petrified alligator jaw!;" "I found a dinosaur jaw;" "I found a petrified eye ball!...it's from a real reptile!;" "I found a small bird's jaw that had teeth." Think of donuts stacked..., now slice them at an angle from top to bottom. When you look at the photo, you can see how people convince themselves of the above.

Many crinoids of different sizes and angles can be formed into a single stone. Thank goodness for the crynoids! I can't wait to hear this year's claims. I enjoy these stones as much as I enjoy watching the chick-a-dees. (See photo 14.)

Crinoid stem fragments have a hollow five raised star shaped center. When this center was found free of shale Native Americans strung them on cords for beads.

Diamonds

Yes, I said diamonds! The Great Lakes region is the

largest diamond field in the United States. Northern Canada has large diamond deposits, so it makes sense that the glaciers carried diamonds down to what is now Lake Michigan.

The diamonds are found in a path two hundred miles wide that runs from Iowa on the west to Ohio on the east. The largest diamonds have been found in Wisconsin near Milwaukee. The largest that I know of, a 21 and a quarter carat diamond, was found near Theresa, Wisconsin. One found near Eagle, Wisconsin, in the southeast part of the state, weighed almost 16 carats. A stone of almost 6 carats was found near Saukville, which is north of Milwaukee. A diamond of nearly 3 carats was found in Dane County, near Madison, Wisconsin. Southwest of Milwaukee, near Burlington, a diamond slightly larger than two carats was found. Fairly close to Manitowoc, a large group of relatively small diamonds were found. In Michigan the largest stone of nearly 10 carats was found near Dowagiac, which is not far from Warren Dunes State Park in the southwest part of Michigan.

Diamonds have been found in at least 6 other Michigan locations, and I've heard of others being found along the shores, but they wouldn't tell me where, and who could blame them! Iowa produced a green diamond said to have been larger than a pea. Illinois, as far as I know, has produced only one diamond. A 6 carat stone was found near Milford, Ohio. Diamonds have been found in thirty locations in Indiana. Five of them ranged in size from 3 to nearly 5 carats. Since most of these stones are just to the east, west or south of Lake Michigan, it seems probable that there are many more diamonds lying unrecognized on Lake Michigan beaches.

Diamonds tend to look frosty and oily. They may or may not have crystal faces. A perfect crystal is unlikely, but a perfect crystal will have 8 faces and 6 points, an octahedral shape. Wisconsin diamonds have a dodecahedral shape instead. If you find a small stone that reflects like feldspar and it is very, very hard (will scratch anything), it could be a diamond (note: wet/dry sandpaper will scratch any stone on the beach, except a diamond).

Diamonds have a perfect cleavage plane and will reflect light off of these planes. When I told a lady about diamonds being found on Lake Michigan, she said with a surprised look, "That's what my father meant when he told me every once in awhile Lake Michigan will cough up a diamond." Who knows? You just may be lucky. (See photo 15.)

Favosite fossils

These fossils will look like a lot of miniature round circles from the top end and many needle-like structures from the side. Think if you had a fist full of sewing needles and you rounded them into a stone. When you look down on the end you'd see round circles, and from the side the long tubes. Favosite fossils have been called by many people "miniature" Petoskey stones, because the eye chambers look the same but smaller. I have heard some people say, "I found a Petoskey stone, but it did not finish growing." I was told by the late Donna Davidson that Michigan has about 26 different corals that can be found. This includes varieties within each species, like the numerous variety of roses. Favosite fossils are a type of petrified coral. They are found in the same limestone as Petoskey stones. You usually will find one favosite fossil for every two or three Petoskey stones. However, on some of the more popular beaches where the Petoskey stones have been picked up, people are now picking up this fossil instead. (See photo 16.)

Feldspar

Feldspar comes in a variety of colors, but primarily pink and white. I have also seen a yellow one. The body of feldspar is normally one color not multiple colors. Feldspar looks very similar to quartz, but it is not. You can tell the difference by the sheen that feldspar puts off in the light. This sheen is seen better when the rock is dry and you have a bright sunny day. If you hold the stone at an angle to your eye, it will reflect light back almost like a mirror. This is because feldspar has a cleavage plane from which the light is reflecting. This is hard to capture on camera, but you can notice how the bottom half of the stone is shinier. (See photo 17.)

Fern Creek tillite

Fern Creek tillite comes from around Norway, Michigan, and is, like the Gowganda tillite, about 2.4 billion years old. It is essentially restricted to the west shore of Lake Michigan. It contains a more random assortment of pebbles than the other two tillites. (See photo 18.)

Frankfort green

The rich green stones found along the shoreline near Frankfort, Michigan, are actually pieces of slag (glass) produced from the smelting of iron ore. The depression of 1890 shut down most of the smelters along the lake and most never reopened. The slag found along the lake is thus more than 100 years old. This glass rounded to pebbles will have a lot of air bubbles in it, creating little holes. (See photo 19.)

Fulgurites

Fulgurites are a reminder from God that "I can create or destroy instantly." In this case it is a creation. A fulgurite is the result of a direct lightning strike into the sand. It instantly fuses the sand, turning it into glass and leaving a hollow center. Fulgurites can form different colors depending on the minerals in the sand. Fulgurites are very rare and are usually found on the higher sand banks. If you spot an unusual impact in the sand, dig down on each side very carefully and maybe you'll find one. They can be as fragile as fine china and break up very easily. This is why the larger pieces have more value. Lightning is estimated to be hotter than the sun's surface, creating more than a billion watts of power. Sand and stones are fused directly to the unusual shape. (See photos 20, 21.)

Greenstones–Michigan's State Gem

Although it is very, very rare to find greenstones in Lake Michigan (along with datolite, copper, silver, gold and diamonds), they are Michigan's state gem stone. A gem stone is a specific combination of elements that is rare in nature. If you are a gold-panner or looking through the small pebbles on the shoreline and come across a green colored stone with a turtle shell pattern, hold on to it. Greenstone (scientific name: Chlorastrolite) is a fibrous material. The crystals in greenstone line up parallel. Light reflects off each individual crystal in unison, creating a chatoyancy. This reflection phenomenon can be seen in the gem stone material tiger-eye as well. You can create chatoyancy by taking a spool of thread and moving it up and down in a bright light. The light will reflect off each thread separately, but it is still viewed as one spool. (See photos 22, 23.)

Granite

If you found a colorful rock with many colors in it, you probably found granite or what farmers sometimes call, fieldstone. Fireplaces, counter tops and landscaping boulders are often made of granite because there is so much of it. The multiple colors in granite come from the minerals attaching to each other as they are cooling. These attaching minerals create "crystals" inside the magma. Each crystal from a different mineral make-up gives you the different colors. These crystals will normally be freckle to dime size. Not always, but granite from the Great Lakes tends to be pink, red, white and/or black. The pink is feldspar; white is quartz; and the black is mica. **Note:** you will probably not find pure mica on the beaches as it is too soft to withstand wave action. (See photo 24.)

Gold

Gold can be panned from the glacial deposits along the lake and from streams that enter the lake. Gold, being heavy, sinks to the bottom of any disturbed sediment that contains it, until it hits bedrock. It moves down the bedrock becoming lodged in joints in the bedrock.

Panning the debris from such joints can produce gold dust. Large nuggets, or even small ones, are unlikely. I suspect, based on conversations I have had with enthusiastic gold panners and the gold I have purchased from them, that you will find about fifty cents worth of gold per hour of work. It is something to do for recreation rather than for money. In about 160 hours of panning, with a little luck, you might be able to find enough gold to make, with the help of a jeweler, a ring for your girlfriend or wife. This can also be a fantastic family activity, and there's no doubt that if you found enough to make a ring, it would be the perfect gift!

When you are on Lake Michigan, the further inland you move, the better odds you'll have of finding gold in a river or stream. (See photo 25.)

The following is a listing of places where gold is said to have been panned from glacial gravel as listed in *Gold in Michigan*, References and Photocopies of Selected Out-or-print publications of the Michigan DNR Geological Survey Division:

Maple River, Ionia County
Lowell, Kent County
Ada Creek, Kent County
Grand River, below Lyons, Ionia County
Flat River, Ontonagon County
Iron River, Marquette County
Ishpeming, Marquette County
Birmingham, Oakland County
Union City Branch, to the S.E. and S.W.
Marcellus, St. Joseph County
Burr Oak, St. Joseph County (pyrites likely)
Grand Haven, Ottawa County
Allegan, Allegan County
Greenville, Montcalm County

Howard City, Montcalm County
County Line, Newaygo County
Muskegon River, Newaygo County
Whitehall, Oceana County
White River, Oceana County
Elbridge, Park, June 7, 1906
Little Sable River, Manistee County
West Summit, Wexford County
Manistee River, Manistee and Wexford counties
Walton, Kalkaska County
Rapid River, Kalkaska, Kalkaska County
Leelanau County, near Lake Michigan
Antrim County, same river (nuggets, reliable)
Boyne River, Charlevoix County
Little Traverse, Emmet County
Victoria Copper Mine (large nugget),
    Keewenau at the tip
Ishpeming district, near gold mines
At points south of Gogebic Iron Range

Gowganda tillite

Gowganda tillite is of the same age and from the same area as pudding stone. It has a dark gray matrix in which round, attractive pebbles of granite are embedded. It can be found on the northeast shore of Lake Michigan. (See photo 26.)

Horn coral

Horn corals are easy to identify if they are a complete specimen without waves eroding away the natural shape. They will have a horn shape, larger at one end and taper to a thin end. Horn coral is more difficult to identify when it is in fragments. End fragments can be identified by their large eye that looks similar to a single "eye" of a Petoskey stone. Fragments from the sidewall of this coral can be deceiving, but if you understand the shape and top view of a full piece, you can "put the pieces together." Sidewall fragments will have two characteristics: parallel lines are from fragments found higher up on the coral or a fragment is from a large coral; small corals or the tips will have parallel lines tapering inward to a single point. When a fragment of this coral is found with the lines of the sidewalls exposed through siltstone or shale, it can really fool a person. I have had many peo-

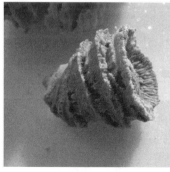

A pristine horn coral that has not been rounded

Horn coral will have a cone shape

ple claim they have found a fossilized bone, only to find out it was the side view of a horn coral. Take a moment to study the photos on page 49. Look at the shape of the coral, where the lines start and end, and what the top looks like. (See photos 27, 28, 29.)

Honeycomb coral

Again this is a coral named by what it looks like. Think of a bee's honeycomb, but the chambers are a little smaller than that of a bee's hive. It is easy to identify a large or small piece. (See photo 30.)

Jasper

Jasper is quartz with enough iron to give it an attractive red or yellow color. It, too, can be cut and polished to produce an attractive inexpensive gem stone. Most come from the iron ore deposits around Marquette. It is around two billion years old. It is more common on the west shore of the lake. Sometimes it is found banded with iron ore or quartz. (See photo 31.)

Lake Superior agate

Lake Superior agates have formed in gas pockets within basalt from quartz brought in by ground water. They can be found on any Lake Michigan beach, but since they are coming from the south shore of Lake Superior, there will be more on the more northernly beaches. They are not common. On a good day on a good beach you might find two or three. Most people go to Lake Superior beaches to look for them, but you will not do much better there. It is best to collect Lake Superior agate while you collect something else of interest. Lake Superior agates are not volcanic, but they were created in volcanic gas pockets by solution of volcanic ash.

Because they have formed in gas pockets they will be potato shaped when whole, but most of what you will find in Lake Michigan will be fragments of a whole agate. Lake Superior agates, or "lakers" as they are sometimes called, are harder than most rocks on the beach. This means the surface of the rock is less resistant to scratches. Thus, agates will have a smooth or "glassy" texture which gives them a greasy feel. Other hard rocks, such a chert, will also have a smooth or greasy feel. However, agates are identified by banding in the stone. They are translucent. By nature, chert is not, but can be, banded, especially around Norwood, Michigan. (There is a lot of banded chert here and novices often think they have found petrified wood.) When an agate is held into the sunlight, you should be able to see into the edges of the rock.

Note: The best way to view transparencey or translucency in a rock is to hold your hand up and out about a foot so as to shade your eyes from direct sun light, then moving the rock from the shadow created by your hand in and out of the sun light.

Still another way to identify an agate is to look for conchoidal chips (like a chip out of a piece of glass). Agates do something unique by which I identify them. The impact from other rocks will create surface cracks that look like thin half moons. One must study the surface very closely to see this. (See photo 33.)

The most sought-after color of the Lake Superior agate is the distinctive red and white banding. (See photo 34.) The red is caused by trace amounts of iron in the stone. This trace amount of iron proved to be very fruitful on a recent hunt for Cathy Gee. Collecting along Lake Michigan between Leland and Glen Arbor, Cathy noticed a little red rock. Liking the color red, she went to pick it up, but discovered it was only the tip of the stone and she had to dig down to uncover it. After unearthing it and realizing its weight, she debated, "do I really want to carry this heavy rock all the way back to the car?" In making this decision she showed it to her friend, Kathy, who was collecting with her. "Cathy! You found an agate.... If you don't want it, I'll carry it back!" Needless to say Cathy carried it back. Not knowing the value of what she had, she brought it to me to have it cut into slabs and made into wind chimes. I politely discouraged her from cutting it up as it was a 6.5pound Lake Superior agate! For a Lake Superior agate to weigh one pound or more is very rare. Serious collectors and museums have paid thousands for 3-5 lbs agates. This 6.5 pound agate was a real treasure from noticing a "little red stone."

6.5 lb Agate found South of Leland near Glen Arbor

Cathy Gee holding a 6.5 lb Lake Superior agate found on Lake Michigan.

One never knows when a rock is going to reveal itself. (See photos 32, 33, 34.)

Leland blue

The rich blue stones found along shoreline near Leland, Michigan, are actually pieces of slag produced by the smelting of iron ore. In 1890 most of the smelters along the lake shut down and never reopened. Thus slag found along the lake is more than 100 years old. The rich blue pieces of glass will be rounded like a rock but will have holes or pores in them. Near this area you can also find a lot of blue chert that looks the same, but it will not have the holes or a glass-like look. Many people pick up both, thinking it is the same stone, but one is a stained chert. The color is only on the surface, caused maybe by some type of stain from its host rock. It also could be the result of weathering or might have something to do with the smelting process that stained the nearby chert. When one is cut open, the inside is brown. (See photo 11.) When the rock is dry, you can separate your chert from the true Leland blue. The chert will have a grayer look when dry. The water will dry out of the holes in the slag (Leland blue) and the holes will be more visible. (See photos 35, 36.)

Lightning stone

These consist of clay cemented into an iron mineral called siderite. These concretions form in part through bacterial activity. They become highly fractured and the fractures fill with calcite brought in by ground water. The result forms lightning-like patterns on a dark background. (See photo 37.)

Marcasite

Marcasite can be found in the Antrim County shale near Atwood, Michigan and Norwood, Michigan. This black shale can produce gold colored balls of marcasite composed of iron and sulfur. It has the same chemical composition as pyrite, but differs from pyrite in its physical characteristics, just as diamond and graphite have the same chemical composition but differ from one another physically. If the ice has split up the shale, you can pick up these round nodules at the water's edge, but much of the time you have to break the shale apart to find the marcasite in between the shale. (See photo 38.)

Misfits

Some misfits are easy to identify on the beach glass, slag,

and fresh pieces of brick and concrete. However, if concrete, asphalt, or bricks have been well tumbled and rounded, they are hard to tell apart from a conglomerate (pebbles cemented together naturally). I have picked up pieces of well rounded brick, thinking it was red jasper, but later realizing it had a "brick" look to it when dry. (See photo 39.)

Moonstone

Michigan or Wisconsin moonstone is named for the state it is found in. The stone is a highly reflective feldspar. It can be found on any beach, but is more common on Upper Peninsula beaches. Cut and polished it makes an attractive, yet inexpensive, gem stone.
(See photo 40.)

Pipe organ coral

Pipe organ coral and horn corals look very, very similar. In fact, if you do not have a large piece or the tip of a horn coral has worn away, you cannot tell them apart. Pipe organ coral grew many tubes next to each other, much like a pipe organ. Horn corals, however, grew as a single coral much like a carrot, the smaller end attached to the sea floor. (See photos 41, 42.)

Petoskey stone

Petoskey stones will have a whitish-gray look when dry and gray when wet. They have "eyes" the size of a pencil. This view is much the same as described above with the favosite fossils. Pretend you have a bundle of pencils this time, looking down into the erasers you will see "eyes." The bottom of this coral (if a full coral head) will look like long pencils going to a single point. Since this is the "hot" stone of the north, it is well worth picking up *The Complete Guide to Petoskey Stones,* a 70 page book all about Petoskey stones and more detailed places to find them. (See photos 43, 44, 45, 46.)

Pudding stone

The pebbles in pudding stone are glacial debris, washed round by an ancient river around 2.4 billion years ago. This river bottom was compressed (metamorphosed) and the round pebbles were "glued" together with white quartz sand. The body of the rock will be white with pebbles ranging in color from red, black and tan. It can be found on the northeastern shore of Lake Michigan, but is much more common on the north east side of the state in Lake Huron. It comes from the vicinity of Elliot Lake in Ontario, Canada.

On a fly-in fishing trip into Canada, I found a spot where I was standing on pudding stone boulders the size of cars! Since my close friends I was with knew what I was about, they strictly warned me that the flight back had limitations of 70 lbs of gear per person. Sadly, I left a lot of pudding stones behind that day. (See photo 47.)

Quartz

Everyone loves to find a round, white quartz rock on the beach, perfectly smooth, and transparent. Pure quartz comes in a varity of colors, but a cream to a yellow color is the most common found. The body of the stone is usually one color, not a variety of colors. Some other colors can be found, such as pure snow white, burgundy, and pink. Do not be fooled with just a pink colored stone, as pink feldspar is common, but a lot less transparent than quartz. Most sand grains are pure quartz. I like to think that quartz is like flour in baking, it is found as a primary ingredient in many other stones like granite, agates, and chert. (See photos 48, 49.)

Rhyolite porphyry

Rhyolite porphyry, had it cooled slowly, would have become granite. As it cooled, large crystals of feldspar and quartz grew within the magma. Then the magma reached the surface as a lava flow and cooled quickly to produce fine crystals. The result is a series of large, attractive crystals frozen in a mass of fine crystals. It comes from the eastern end of the floor of Lake Superior and is probably about two billion years old. It can be found almost without looking on any Lake Michigan shore that has glacial debris. In Wisconsin it is sometimes called driveway rock because boulders of it are used as an accent along driveways.

Other porphyry

Almost any igneous rock can end up with large crystals embedded in a mass of fine ones. There is an almost endless variety of attractive prophyrys on any stony Lake Michigan beach. Sometimes the large crystals spray out from a central point resulting in a flower-like appearance. Green flowers on a dark background are a common type. Green olivine, or peridot, crystals in a dark basalt or gabbro can be found. (See photo 50.)

Sandstone

Sandstone is just what it sounds like. Sand that was pressed together to make stone. It comes in a variety of colors. If you look closely at the stone's surface, it will look like a bunch of sand grains cemented together. Also when the stone is dry, put a couple droplets of water on it, and the water will absorb into the surface almost instantaneously. (See photo 51.)

Stink stone

These stones are just for fun - not much for character and overlooked all the time. They will be cream to white in color with many little holes all over - almost like something brought back from the moon. One day my dear friend and mentor, Vic Nielson, showed me this stone. He broke one open at Peterson Park and had me smell it right away. My eyes watered at the stench of rotten eggs. The gas trapped in this limestone may be hydrogen sulfide. Some rocks will smell stronger than others, depending on how or if the gas has dissipated. Once the rock is broken open, you must smell it right away. (See photo 52.)

REMEMBER- rock shards are sharper than scalpels, a proven fact! People walk the beaches bare foot. If you choose to break open stones, do it in a safe place using safe measures.

Trilobite

Trilobites are usually found on flat, recently split stone surfaces. The beach where stones are worn round is not the place to find many. Quarries where rock has been recently broken are better, but permission to enter these is seldom given. The most commonly found Devonian trilobite is *Phacops rana*. The most commonly found Silurian trilobite which is Wisconsin's State Fossil, is Calamene. Dalmanites are also common in Silurian rock. (See photo 53.)

Unakite

Unakite is an orange or pinkish granite containing intrusions (sometimes streaks) of light-green epidote. It is mined in New England states as an inexpensive gem stone. It can be found on both sides of the lake, and some of what is found along the lake is the best there is. I know of two instances in which it has been mounted in karat gold jewelry. (See photos 54, 55.)

Layman's Rock Identification

Lake Michigan is one of the most unique places in the world to collect rocks. Nowhere else in the world do you find glacial deposits from such a vast area and such variety of local bedrock in one lake. And in a pile, they are confusing (see the picture of Dixie cup collection before and after it was sorted). As Bruce has mentioned, you cannot scratch Canadian Shield rocks with a knife. What I am about to describe is not always 100% accurate, but it will get you to identify your rocks a lot easier. Color is not always a sure way for identification, but it is the easiest, and I'd like to start here.

Get your rock finds wet–it is always more enjoyable looking through them. Take all the grayish black, gray, and cream colored rocks and put them in one pile. Do not put in this pile any rocks that are transparent or ones you cannot scratch with a knife (steel-hardness 5.5). Most local fossils and bedrock are this color and less than a 5.5 in hardness. You now have 50% of your stones identified!

This pile should contain the local bed rock that was here prior to the glaciers bringing down new and different material from Canada. This pile should contain limestones and dolomite, including most fossils, Petoskey stones, favosite fossils, horn corals, limestone, and Cladoporia.

The second pile should contain all the variety of colored rocks, rocks primarily from Canada. Take this pile and break it up in two. Take all the rocks that are a solid color and put them in a pile (you usually have quartz and jasper and chert in this pile). The multiple-colored pile that is left can be tricky, but pull out all the granites (see the picture or think of granite counter tops or a fieldstone fireplace). Granites will be spotted with multiple colors. The spots will be from freckle to dime size depending on the size of the crystal. My guess is by now, using the descriptions and pictures above, you should have an idea about 90% of the rocks you have picked up.

Again, this is not fool-proof. One major flaw is the corals described can also be agatized. That is, instead of the shell being replaced with calcite during petrifaction, it was replaced with quartz. I have seen Petoskey stones and other fossils be replaced by quartz. You then would not be able to scratch these with a knife.

About 50% of the rocks on Lake Michigan are sedimentary including dolomite, shale and limestone.

This is a "high bank" area near Peterson Park
on the Leelanau Peninsula.

Walking the Lake Shoreline – Your Legal Rights

In Michigan, the Supreme Court has recently ruled that the
beach, so long as you stay between the low water and high
water marks, is not private property but rather accessible to
anyone who wishes to walk the beach. Once on the beach,
you can walk as far as you wish. Personally, I stay away from
areas where there are a lot of houses right down by the lake.
There are many "high bank" areas where the shoreline rises
too abruptly, leaving no place between the lake and the bluff
above to build a house. I prefer these beaches. Also, I do not
wish to walk through a summer BBQ, unless I am invited.

The Story Behind the Leland Blue and Frankfort Green

One of the most frequently asked "what-kind-of-stone-is-this" questions has to do with blue, green, purple and black glass-like stones found along the lake. These stones are sometimes cut, polished and fashioned into pendants and rings, complete with karat gold mountings, and then sold to tourists and others. The stones found near Leland, Michigan, are often referred to simply as Leland blue. Those found near Frankfort are called Frankfort green. They look important, and in a peculiar way, they are important. These are actually pieces of slag produced by the smelting of iron ore.

In 1844 iron ore was discovered by a U.S. surveyor near Marquette, Michigan. A mining company claimed and bought a square mile of land in the area for two dollars and fifty cents an acre. A smelter was built, and the first iron ore was produced in 1848. Smelting furnaces in the next 50 years proliferated until there were 29 in the Upper Peninsula alone. I have been unable to learn how many there were on the Lower Peninsula, but there was one at Petoskey, one at Leland, one at Elk Rapids and one at Elberta. It is likely there was also one at Charlevoix. If Leland and Elk Rapids had one, it seems probable that nearly every little village along the lake had one.

To smelt the iron ore, a mix of powdered iron ore, charcoal and dolomite was dropped into the furnace

Two restored iron smelters at Fayette on the Garden
Peninsula of the Upper Peninsula

from the top. Dolomite was used as a flux. A flux is used
to lower melting points. (Salt is in some sense a flux for
ice.) The charcoal burned by taking oxygen, not from the
air, but rather from the iron ore, which is an iron oxide.
The furnace was tapped at the base where the melted
iron flowed out. Iron ore contains quartz as an impuri-
ty. Melted quartz is glass. The quartz and dolomite rose
to the top of the furnace to an opening where this slag
was drawn off. I would hate to accuse anyone of litter-
ing without knowing for sure, but my feeling is that the
slag was disposed of by dumping it into the lake. At
Elberta, formerly South Frankfort, Little Betsie Bay was
filled to a distance of 100 feet offshore with slag. More was
dumped as railroad ballast along the railroad track leading
out of Elberta. Along the former tracks, now a bike path,
slag is frequently found today near Crystal Lake.

Color

1. The color in this photo contains every color, but a true purple. These were picked up in a two hour trip near Leland, Michigan.

Variety

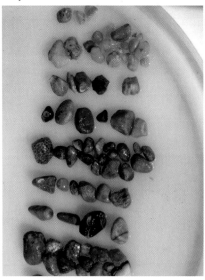

2. Colors and variety in one Dixie cup, unsorted

3. 16 flavors in a Dixie cup, sorted

4. Basalt is black to dark green in color

5. Basalt with quartz veins

6. A piece of fractured basalt that
is filled with quartz

7. Full brachiopods that have not
been beach washed

8. Chain coral is tan with white chain lines running through it

9. Chain coral cut two different ways can produce two totally different patterns

10. Chert will have concoidle fractures (dish-like fractures)

11. Blue chert found near Leland – notice the cut pieces show that it is only a stain on the outside

12. Cladopora (polished and natural)

13. Copper

14. Crinoids–the stones on the left are pristine pieces that have not been beach washed. The stones on the right are more commonly found on the beach.

15. Diamonds–notice the greasy or shiny look when they are dry–note the triangle shape to the top one

16. Favosite fossil (Charlevoix stone) will have small eyes much like a Petoskey stone

17. Feldspar is normally pink and will reflect sun light best when dry

18. Fern Creek tillite

19. Frankfort green is a green slag with many tiny bubbles in the surface

20. An excellent example of a fulgurite that has been split in half– notice the glass-like inside

21. The end of a fulgurite showing the hollow end lightning left behind

22. Greenstones are green with a turtle shell pattern–most are pea size or smaller

23. Greenstones cut and polished

24. Granite will usually be pink, white and black in color

sand

gold dust

25. Gold dust you'll find panning is pepper flake size–large nuggets are very rare

26. Gowganda tillite

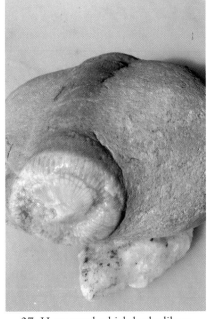

27. Horn coral which looks like a petrified bone

28. A natural horn coral with one that has been sliced and polished. Compare these to the horn coral fragements.

29. The three pieces (upper left) are from a horn coral cut two different ways. The rest are beach washed fragments.

30. Honeycomb coral (or favosite) will look like the honey comb from a bee's nest

31. Jasper often has a burgundy to red appearance

32. 6.5 lb Lake Superior agate with the end polished (found in Lake Michigan)

33. Moon-like chips commonly found on agates

34. Classic color of Lake Superior agates (they are not limited to this red and white color)

35. Leland blue slag has a very intense rich blue color

36. When dry, it's easier to tell Leland blue (upper three) apart from blue chert. Notice the glossy holes in Leland blue.

37. Lightning stones

38. Marcasite found in the Antrim Shale near Norwood, Michigan

39. Misfits of Lake Michigan can be beach glass, slag, bricks, asphalt, and cement

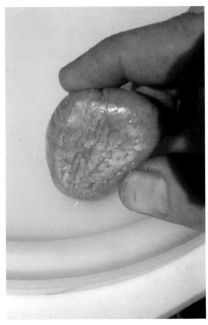

40. Moonstone is highly reflective feldspar, containing fibers like those found in fiber optics cable

41. Pipe organ coral

42. Pipe coral head

43. 14k Petoksey stone with diamond set in the "eye"and black onyx inlay

44. Petoskey stones will have eyes that show up more when wet or polished

45. Petoskey stones cut two different ways show different patterns

46. Petoskey stone (upper right) shows the white chalk marks next to a lime stone–see page 69 for story

47. Pudding stone will have red, black and white stones "cemented" together with quartz

48. Quartz will usually have one body color, cream or white

49. Quartz when sliced is very transparent

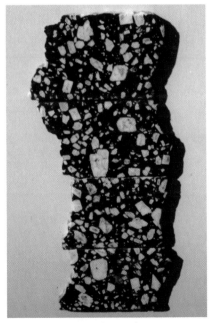

50. Basalt porphyry

51. Sandstone will look like sand grains cemented together

52. Stink stone will be cream color with many small holes

53. Trilobite

54. Unakite will be pink with green lines

55. Unakite set in 14k with diamond accent

A. What do you see?

B. What do you see?

C. What do you see?

D. What do you see?

E. What do you see?

F. What do you see?

Answers:
A. Petoskey stone
B. Red jasper next to favosite fossil
C. Horn coral
D. A horn coral
E. Unakite
F. Four stink stones

The furnaces ran night and day, never shutting down. To shut down required a time-consuming and expensive reheating of the furnace. At Elberta they had two smelting furnaces and produced 40 tons of iron per day. The needed charcoal was produced by burning wood in a kiln shaped like a bee hive. At Elberta they had 22 charcoal kilns, each of which held one hundred cords of wood. It took an acre of hardwood to produce two tons

The source of Leland blue and Frankfort green

of iron. To run the Elberta furnaces for a year required the leveling of 7,300 acres of hardwood forest. Hardwood made the best charcoal. Wood cutters were paid about 80 cents a cord for wood. England, once the leading iron producer in the world, was reduced to a forest of stumps by the eighteenth century. This led to the use of coal for smelting, but coal contains sulfur, resulting in brittle iron.

The depression of 1890 shut down most of the

Miniaturized restored version of a charcoal kiln at Fayette
on the Garden Peninsula of the Upper Peninsula

smelters along the lake and most never reopened. This
makes the slag found along the lake more than 100 years
old. Two of the early smelters in the Upper Peninsula,
along with the company town, have been restored at
Fayette on the Garden Peninsula. Across the bay from
Fayette you will see a great cliff of Silurian Niagaran
dolomite which is still quarried elsewhere for flux. Fayette
Village is well worth a visit.

Driftwood has piled up the stones–a good place to look

Tips on Successful Outings

- Start out early in the morning, the water is calmer.
- Right after or during light rain, all the rocks will be wet.
- Spring or fall storms will turn over new and undiscovered material to look at.
- Under flat rocks or in between large rocks is a good place to look.
- Trees that are leaning into the water from undermining wave action–get inside the branches and look. The rocks will pile up here and most people will not go there.
- Rocks also tend to pile up in front of drift wood and large objects on the beach–dig through these piles. Much is undiscovered and under the surface and the rocks will be wet.
- A backpack can carry food and water in one direction and larger rocks back.

- Walk down the beach a ways without picking up rocks, then turn around heading back to your destination while picking. The carrying is easier one direction, and you will be back at your car with the bucket full. (I should take this one to heart more often.)
- Label your collections with date and place of where you found your stones, especially if you are on vacation - it is easy to forget. It will help with future rock hunts. Gems are more valued to collectors knowing the location.
- Use square pails (like cat litter pails). They are easier to carry.

Finding More Petoskey Stones

Petoskey stones are easier to identify in the water, but once you train your eye on what to look for when dry, YOU WILL always find them - wet, dry, lake, gravel pit, driveway... places where hundreds of people look or tens of thousands of people have walked. The winter of 2006, I walked through Traverse City's Holiday Inn parking lot. I am comfortable to say in one year's time over a 100,000 people walk through this parking lot, especially because of the National Cherry Festival. This hotel has been there for decades, so much so that the gravel around the trees (note: most large parking lots contain gravel around decorative trees and bushes) had been walked on so much, the baseball-size rocks were polished and pushed into the ground like cobble stones. I noticed a 5-inch Petoskey stone right there. How did over a million people miss it and I picked it up? What am I looking for that most people are not seeing? Simple, the white "chalk marks." The calcite, which replaced the living coral, is soft and will leave white chalk marks on Petoskey stones when impacted by other rocks. When dry, limestone and Petoskey stones are the same color and are difficult for the eye receptors to separate, unless you are looking for these chalk marks. You may say, "well, I can't spot a Petoskey stone dry," but now you know why you can find them. You have trained your eye.

It may be difficult to see in the photos, but next to the limestone you can see how Petoskey stones will show white spots, as if someone took a piece of chalk and hit it against the stone. (See photo 46.)

When people see all the Petoskey stones I have found they always ask, "where did you get your Petoskey stones?" They lean forward a bit and glance around as if someone is listening and I am about to share a big secret. I get a blank stare when I reply, "I find them all over." I have found Petoskey stones on all beaches, in parking lots such as at Home Depot, Sears and K-mart, gravel piles waiting to build the road, septic gravel, roof top gravel, construction sites and many, many other places. I'm just always looking. The person who poses the question always gives me a disappointed look like

I'm not telling them the truth. I will now just answer with a smile, "It's all in the *Lake Michigan Rock Picker's Guide*. I have a copy, would you like one?"

Jellyfish and corals are among the most ancient organisms alive today. They split and went their separate ways, one drifting, the other fixed to the sea floor, perhaps two thirds of a billion years ago or more.

A Quick Guide to Polishing Petoskey Stones

To polish Petoskey stones and other fossils composed of calcite, put them in a rolling tumbler for two days with 600 grit. Take them out, rinse them off and polish them with a cloth buff or an electric motor and a polishing compound called ZAM, available at most rock shops. A minute or two of buffing should make them shine. They can be drilled using a drill press and a solid carbide drill bit.

Gunflint chert is among the oldest rock known, dating back about three and one-half billion years. Fossil bacteria are found in it .

Geological Time in a human "life expectancy" 70 year increments (depending on your beliefs)

United States was founded	3.3 life expectancies ago
Birth of Christ	29
200 B.C.	31.9
Petoskey coral heads formed	5 million
1 Billion years ago	14.3 million life times!

Petoskey stone coral was extinct before dinosaurs were born. If you have found a Petoskey stone you have found a coral that is older than a dinosaur!

How to Pan for Gold

Steps:

1. Get a gold pan from a rock and mineral store or from the web. Look for one that has riffles - bars or slats - and a catch hole in the bottom, since these help the gold to separate from other particles more easily. Plastic pans are generally preferred over metal pans because they are lighter, have shallower angles (to reduce the risk of the gold being tossed out of the pan), and because gold is easier to spot against plastic than against shiny metal.

2. Before you begin, familiarize yourself with the recreational prospecting regulations of the area in which you wish to pan for gold.

3. Choose a location along a river or creek to pan. The further away from the mouth of the river or steam, the better. Places where the water slows down noticeably, such as behind sandbars or large rocks, are usually good spots for panning. You can also ask state or national park officials for recommendations about the best places to pan and the park's policies.

4. Fill the pan almost to the top with sand from the edge of the creek or river. Try sand from various depths. Use a shovel to dig deeper.

5. Dip the pan's edge into the stream and fill it with water.

6. Hold the pan with one hand and swirl it to mix the sand. Any gold will start settling toward the bottom of the pan.

7. Swirl the pan faster. You will lose some of the water, along with lighter particles of sand as you go.

8. Begin scraping the top sand out of the pan with your free hand.

9. Continue until much of the pan is empty, leaving only small bits of gold - if you're lucky - in a little water.

10. Use tweezers or a pipette to retrieve tiny gold particles and pick out larger samples with your fingers.

11. Keep all gold samples in plastic vials or sample bottles.

Tip:
Try running the sand through a sieve or screen to get rid of larger particles before placing it in your gold pan.

Pyrite, or fool's gold, looks like the real thing but has no value. There's lots of it out there, and it's fun to find even though it won't make you rich. To make sure you've found gold and not fool's gold, rub the stone against something white, like porcelain. If it leaves a black streak, it's fool's gold. If it leaves a yellow streak, it's gold. Gold is also much softer than fool's gold. Gold can be found farther downstream from its usual source after heavy rains, since the rush of water dislodges it and carries it away.

> When struck with a hammer, pyrite will shatter.
> Gold will flatten!

Gravel pits
Beaches are the easy, beautiful places to select attractive and interesting stones, but they are not the only places. The going price for a full bucket of gravel, hand-selected

by yourself at a gravel pit, is 2 dollars. You can get a ton for about 20 dollars. This will be the same glacial gravel that you would find along the lake. This assumes that you live in the Midwest north of the Ohio and Missouri rivers, which were created along the edge of the Illinoisan ice sheet, the largest of the ice sheets.

The rock from gravel pits will not be as round and smooth as that along the lake and so will require a little more work to polish, but not a lot more. If you live along the Mississippi River, keep in mind that when the east end of Lake Superior was blocked by the glacier, great volumes of melt water poured down the St. Croix River and into the Mississippi, carrying along what must have been a few hundred tons of Lake Superior agates. Gravel dredged from the Mississippi River will contain many Lake Superior agates. As a boy I walked home from school along a road covered with gravel from the Mississippi and could always find a Lake Superior agate or two on the way home.

Fossils

It is beyond the scope of this book to cover more than the most common fossils found along the lake. To check up on fossils other than these, I recommend that you refer to *The Complete Guide to Michigan Fossils* (2006), which is an excellent resource.

Passion of hunting – the rock finds you

Most of the time the rock finds you. Yes, it chooses YOU to be discovered. More times than not, the prize of the day is found when the rock "just jumps out at you." People have found that "prize rock" when they first get out of the car, imbedded in the gravel road a few feet away. Or it is the one that jumped out at you, but you had to get your feet wet to retrieve it. Then there is the classic pocket rock. You are walking down the beach with your pail, it becomes heavy so you pause for a moment to sit down on a large piece of driftwood. You look down... and there! Right there! A perfect rock! A foot away from where you are sitting in plain view, for everyone in the world to see, but you found it and it is now yours. You reach down, pick it up and turn the rock around to notice the stripe that runs all the way through it, and it's your favorite color, green. You proudly put this one in your pocket so it does not get mixed up with the other stones. Being in the pocket also allows you to retrieve it easier and show it off. You now have a pocket rock.

Like many prize finds, I can remember exactly where I found a particular rock, sometimes even down to what kind of a day it was. The point here is that you should do something with that special rock. Many, many rocks sit in a bucket, stored away in the garage only to be pulled out once or twice and glanced through. Enjoy your prize rock while it is in your possession. I encourage you to start a rock garden, polish one side or make a piece of jewelry. Put your mark on it as if to say "I possess this rock. It might have been around for millions of years, but I, John Doe, am enjoying it now." Notice the piece of jewelry made from the unakite stone in photo 55. A gentleman had this made from his wife's favorite stone.

Rock Snoids- Be aware

Rock snoids looking for people

Rock snoids are believed to be a living rock with very finicky character. On a good day, they are responsible for putting a perfect rock on the beach just ahead of you. However, these same little creatures are more commonly known to play pranks. When you get a glimpse of a great find right at the water's edge, they are likely to have a wave snatch it away from you, never to be seen again. They are the ones who are primarily responsible for getting your shoes or pant bottoms initially wet. They love to move things or hide them. On the beach, rock snoids are responsible for moving the rock that you have placed on top of a larger one to pick up later. When you return back down the beach you swore you put it right there, but cannot find it. Most of all, they misplace the really cool rock you keep telling others you have found, but cannot find in your collection.

Misfits found on the lake

This may be a good time to talk about misfits in Lake Michigan. Keep in mind, on rare occasions, some unwanted collections containing rocks from other locations have been dumped back into Lake Michigan. One day a lady brought me a very pretty blue and green rock she found in Grand Traverse Bay. It turned out to be a piece of auzrite and malichite from Arizona. She also found a piece of amethyst from Brazil and a few miscellaneous other things in the same area. These pieces had sharp enough edges to identify them as freshly mined pieces and not glacial transports. Although great discoveries, these pieces were not native to Lake Michigan. Black coal, washed concrete, tumbled asphalt, glass, Leland blues, and Frankfort greens are common on Lake Michigan, but still misfits. (See photo 39.)

What to Do with Your Rock Collection

Once you have collected these beautiful rocks, what are you going to do with them? Many people leave them in a container stored away. I encourage you to do something with them!

Many projects can be made without special equipment. Some will require a dremel, diamond tipped drill,

Builder with his mailbox of cemented polished stones

sand paper, or bench grinder. Still others require getting in a little deeper with rock cutting equipment or the help of a professional. Whatever you may choose, the only thing more rewarding than finding a gem is showing it off.

You do not need elaborate polishing equipment to shine rocks. You can go down to the local hardware store and buy a clear coat in the paint department. This can be sprayed on any rock to make them look wet. I prefer the Krylon brand because it dries fast so you can give multiple coats (light spray each time will yield better results), and it will not yellow. Make sure your rocks are clean (24 hours in bleach and water will clean algae) and dry. If you are doing a large project such as mail boxes, lamps, or ash trays, you will want to spray after all the rocks are glued and grouted.

- Rocks can be glued to flat cabinet pulls
- Bell caps (which local rock shops carry) can be glued

to the top of small stones and worn as a pendant
- Lamp finials can be made
- Light pulls
- Light switch plates (with rock cutting equipment)
- Wire wrap trees, with tiny rocks as the leaves
- Candle holders
- Door stops
- Beads can be made (it is very difficult to drill rocks and most drilling is done in China with sonic drills)
- Tiles can be cut for a floor or back splash as accent pieces. Cut and polished into shapes
- Carvings
- Cut and polished into fine jewelry and accented with faceted stones

"We only borrow rocks"
Kevin Gauthier

I've heard of so many collectors speak as if they actually own their rocks. Even I am guilty of this. But, then I remember these rocks were here long before my great, great, great... grandparents were around and they will be here long after my children's children's children have passed. We only borrow rocks. I have heard of rock collections changing hands only to end up in a landfill. I have often wondered about thousands of years from now who will dig up this collection and rediscover it. Wherever your rock ventures take you, keep in mind the treasures on Lake Michigan have been around for a long time. How many rocks have you looked at and disregarded? Who's collection are they in now or are the waves still honing them? I have always liked the obvious single rock, or a very large boulder scenario. Who put it there? Were they planning to come back and get it? Was it the rock snoids? Is it better than the rocks I picked up? Let me go look at it!